Snakes and Lizards

Studies for Wildlife Artists

Photography and Text

by

Al Lodwick

First Edition 2015

ISBN:9781517076283

DEDICATION

To Ann Lodwick, my wife and best friend for nearly thirty-eight years.

ACKNOWLEDGEMENTS

Scott Mies for encouragement and editorial advice.

Tony Krzysik, Ph.D. for identification and fact checking

Rachel Lodwick for the Mieswick, LLC logo.

Victoria Tubbs for the author's photograph.

INTRODUCTION

This book is the result of almost five years of nearly daily photographing nature in the biologically diverse state of Arizona. The ecosystems involved have varied from the Sonoran Desert to the Ponderosa Pine woodlands. Snakes and lizards can be found almost everywhere from the trees overhead to spaces between rocks on the ground.

In my consultations with Tony Krzysik, I learned that there is nothing in Arizona that will stalk humans as prey. In order to become a victim of a reptile in Arizona you have to either be negligent in approaching them or be acting aggressively toward them. (Aggression is a decision that the snake or lizard makes, not the human.)

Gila Monsters and Western Diamondbacks are not included in this book because they are not easily seen by a casual walker and there is an abundance of their photos elsewhere. The pictures were all taken in Arizona while I was on almost daily walks. There were no special set-ups, not even a tripod was used.

Photorealistic wildlife artists face difficulties in depicting everything perfectly because one's memory cannot store all of the details in a fleeting moment. Even one reference photo will fall short of getting everything "just right". The purpose of this book is to supply as many visual details as possible.

The author hopes that non-artists will also enjoy the pictures and learn more about these magnificent snakes and lizards of Arizona.

Al Lodwick
Prescott, Arizona
August 2015

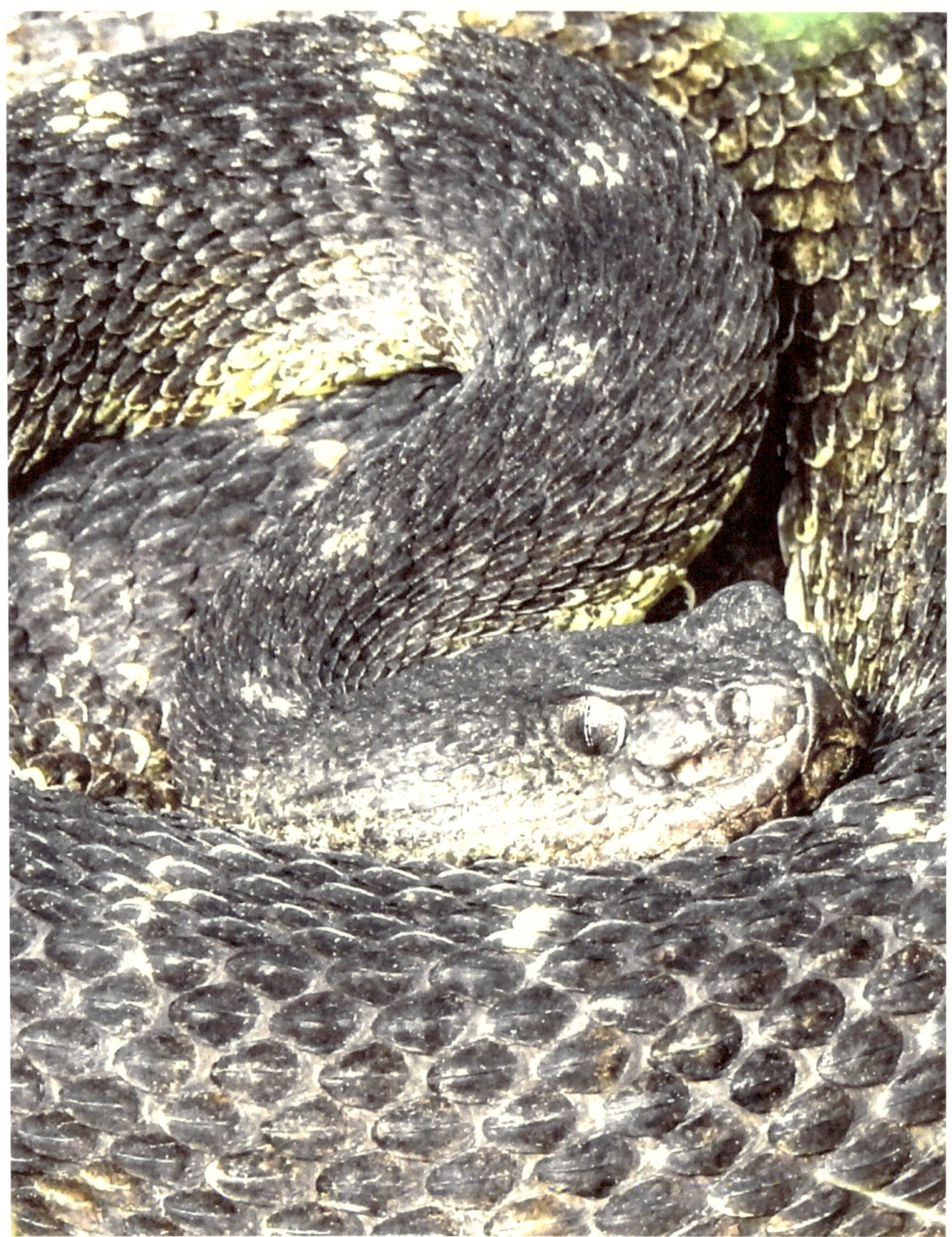

This full-grown adult was about 3 feet long. I watched it crawl along a trail until it found a place at the base of a cottonwood tree to coil and warm up in the morning sun.

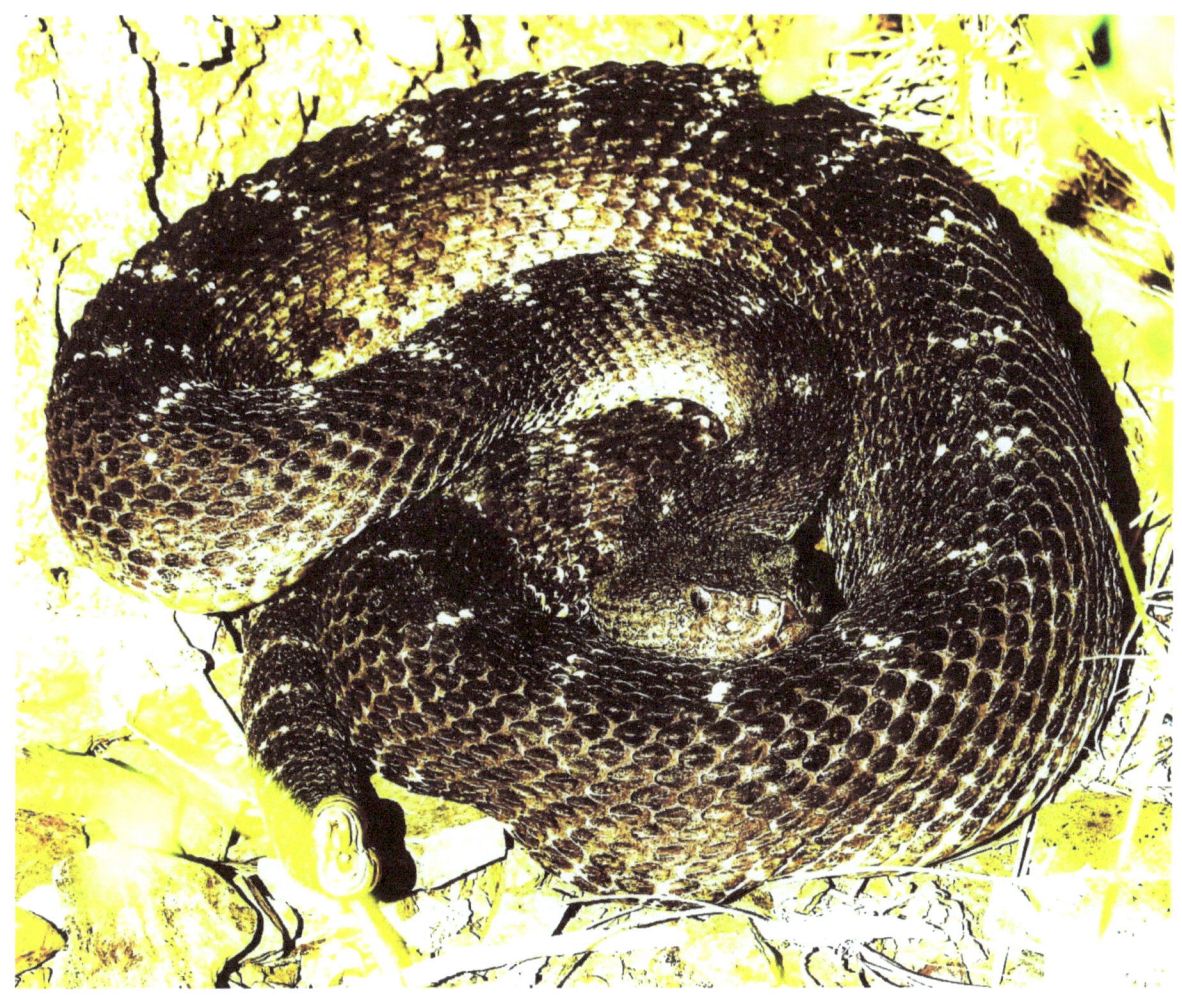

This is the same snake as in the previous photo. They have the ability to change color rather rapidly like a chameleon.

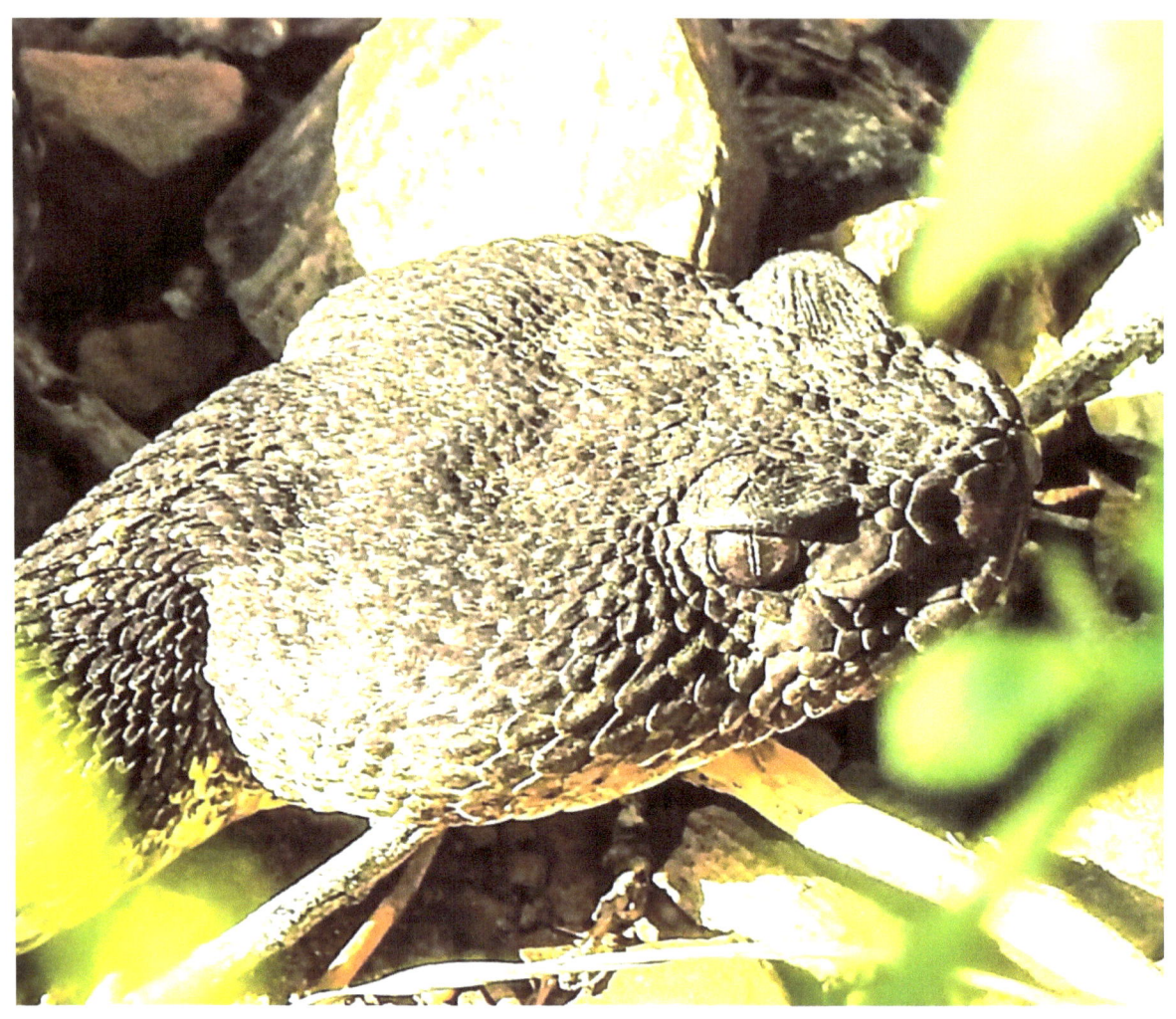

Note the pit in front of the eye. This is an infrared sensor that can detect very small temperature changes. It has one on each side. Even in total darkness it can sense a mammal's motion and strike.

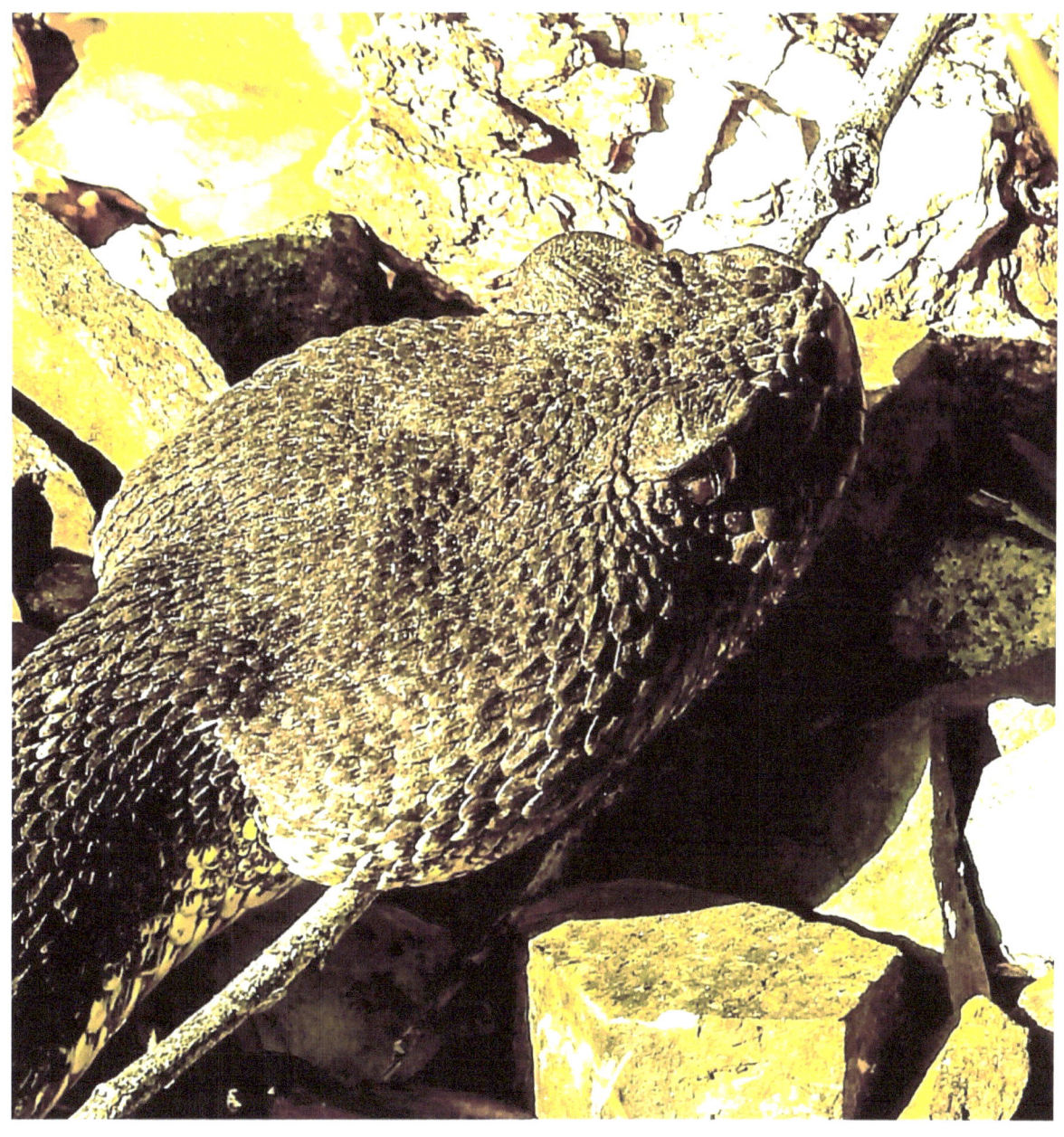

Note the how much larger the head is compared to the body of the snake. It has the ability to unhinge its lower jaw and work a large prey into its mouth with an action similar to walking the jaw bones.

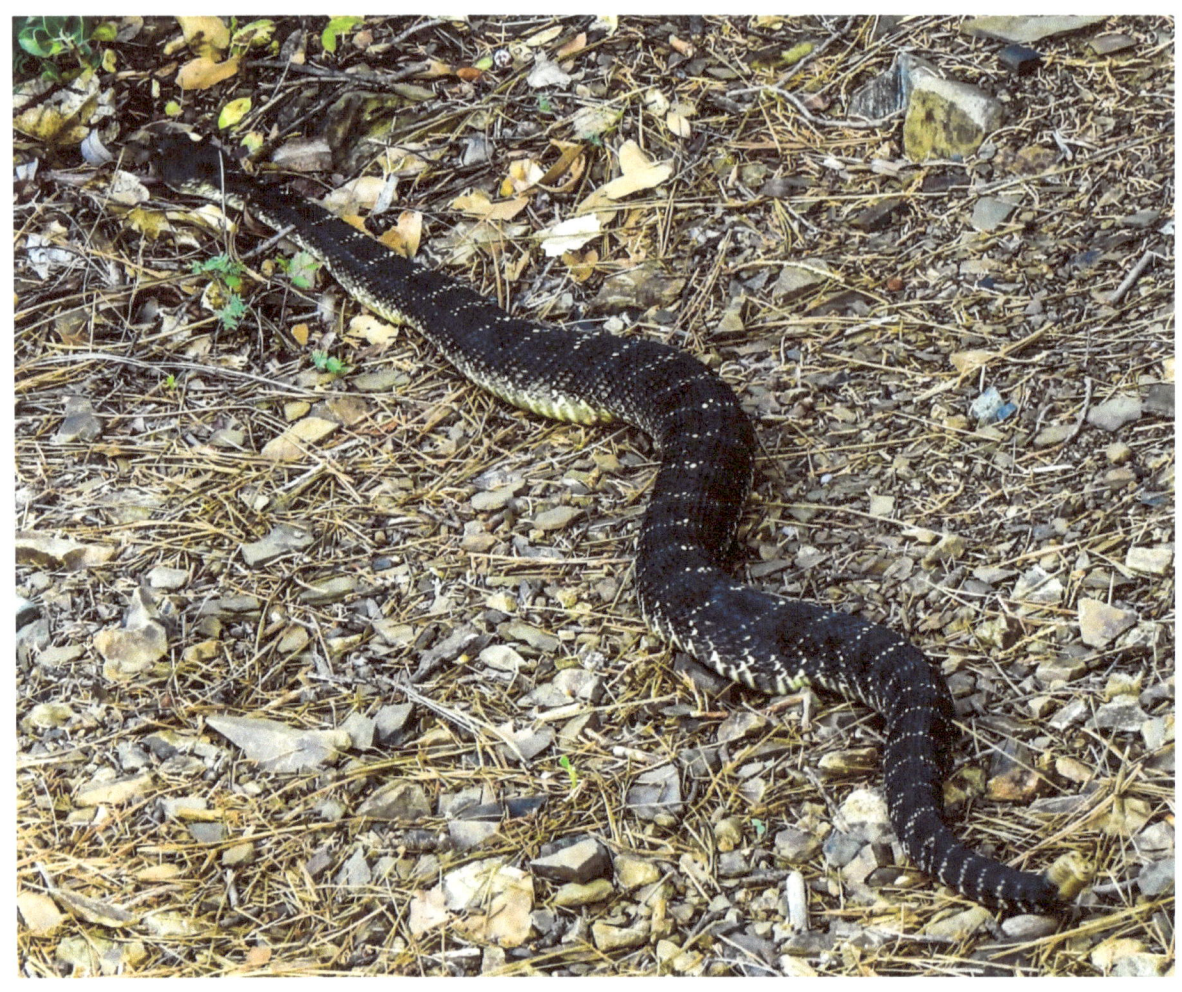

Arizona Black Rattlesnakes may not rattle and do not always bite when someone gets too near. I have witnessed them simply giving a hard slap on the leg of someone who got too close.

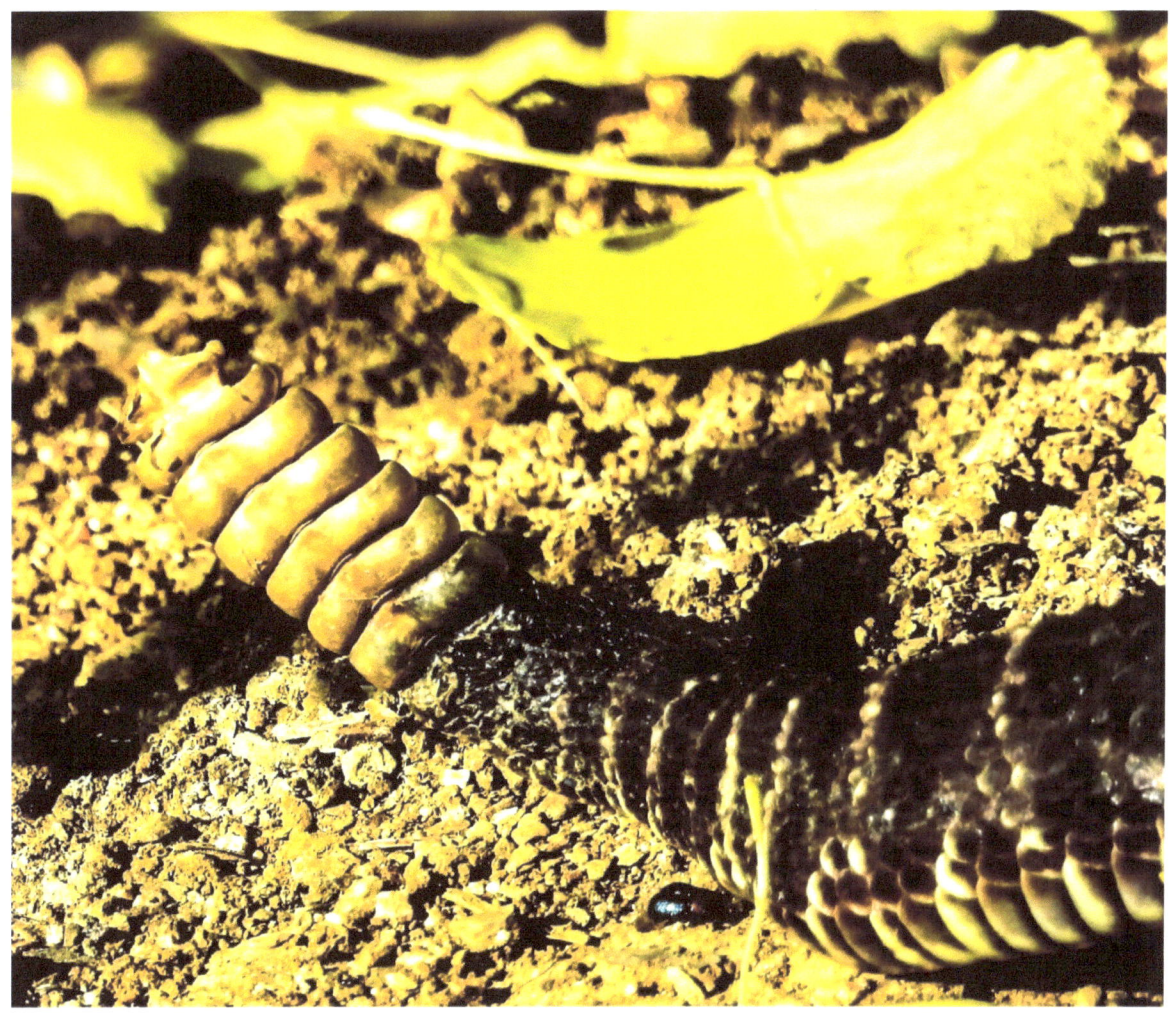

Rattlesnakes do not grow another rattle each year. Instead they add one whenever they shed their skin. This is similar to human growth spurts that do not conform to birthdays.

GOPHER (BULL) SNAKE

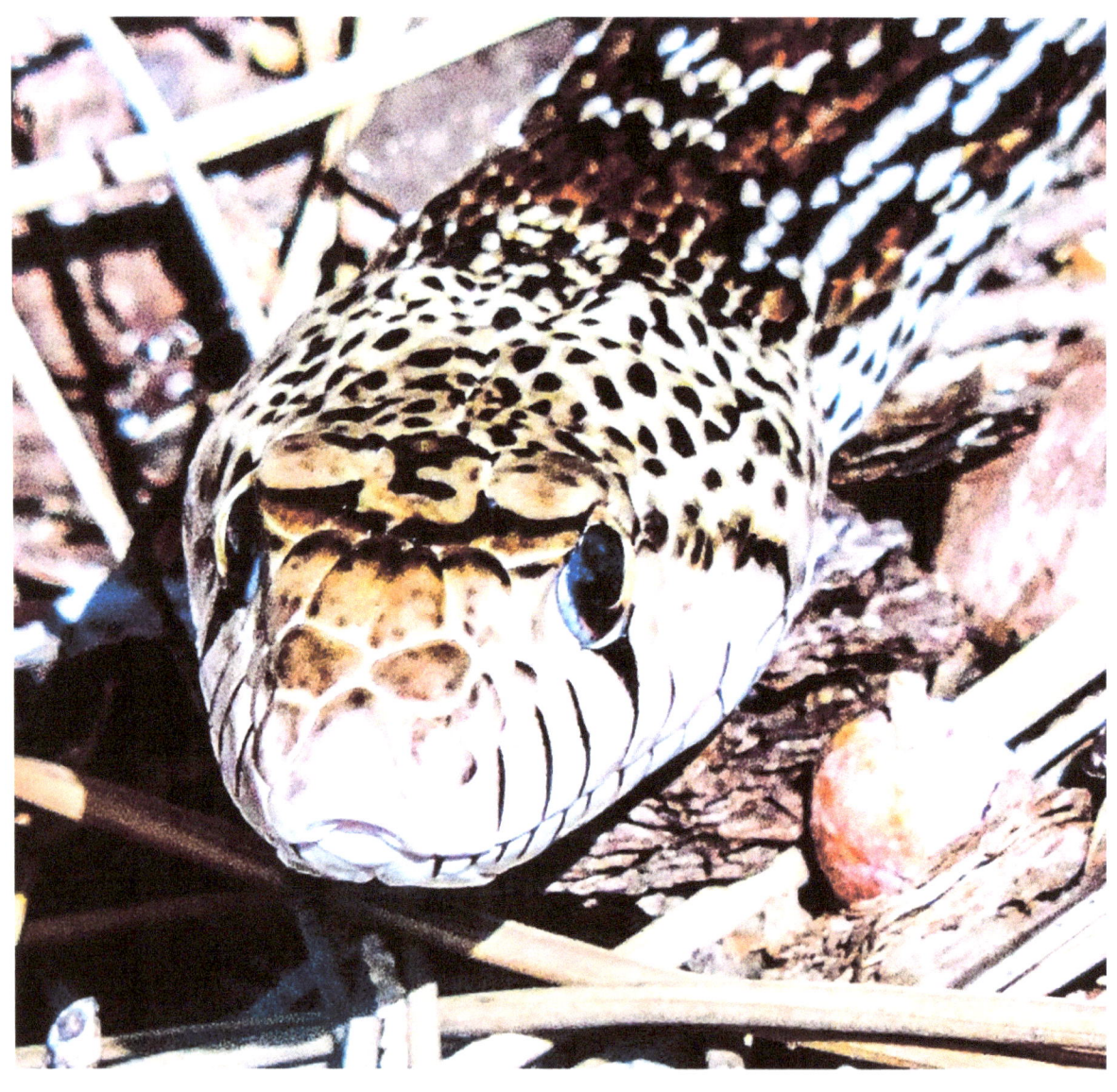

These are not poisonous. Their head is not much wider than their body making is easy to tell them from Diamondbacks. Adults are typically 3 to 7 feet long. They can be quite tolerant of humans.

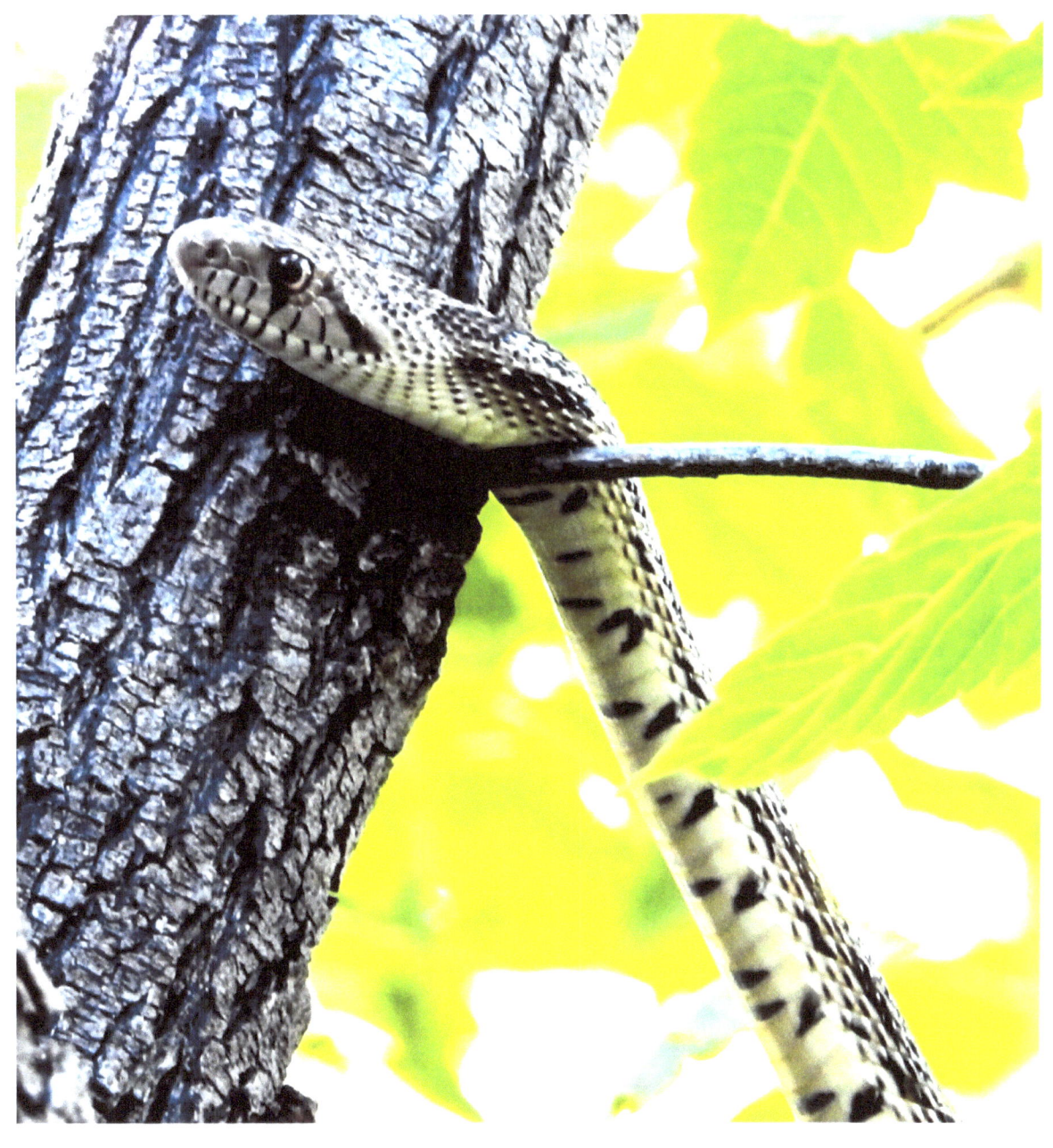

Gopher snakes can easily climb trees. Wild ones live about 15 years. The longest known one in captivity was 33 years. They will eat eggs and young birds.

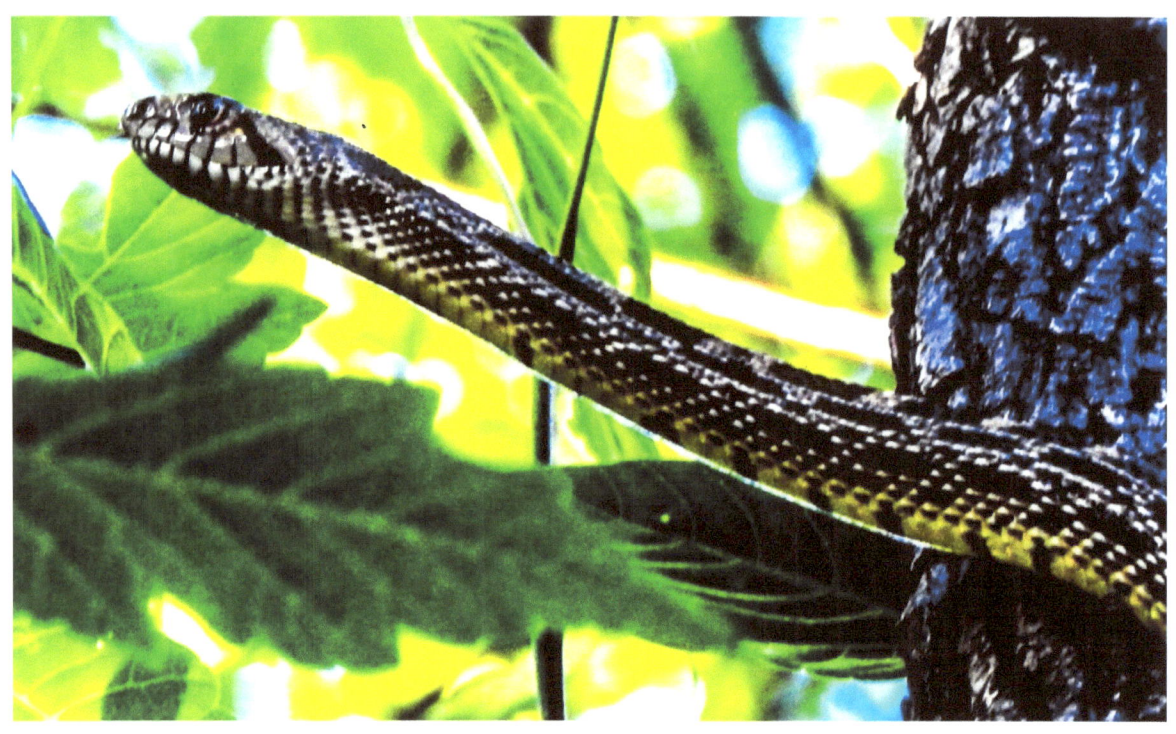

They have been known to coil up and shake their tail in an attempt to neutralize threats by mimicking a rattlesnake. Sometimes they jab with a closed mouth to warn away threats.

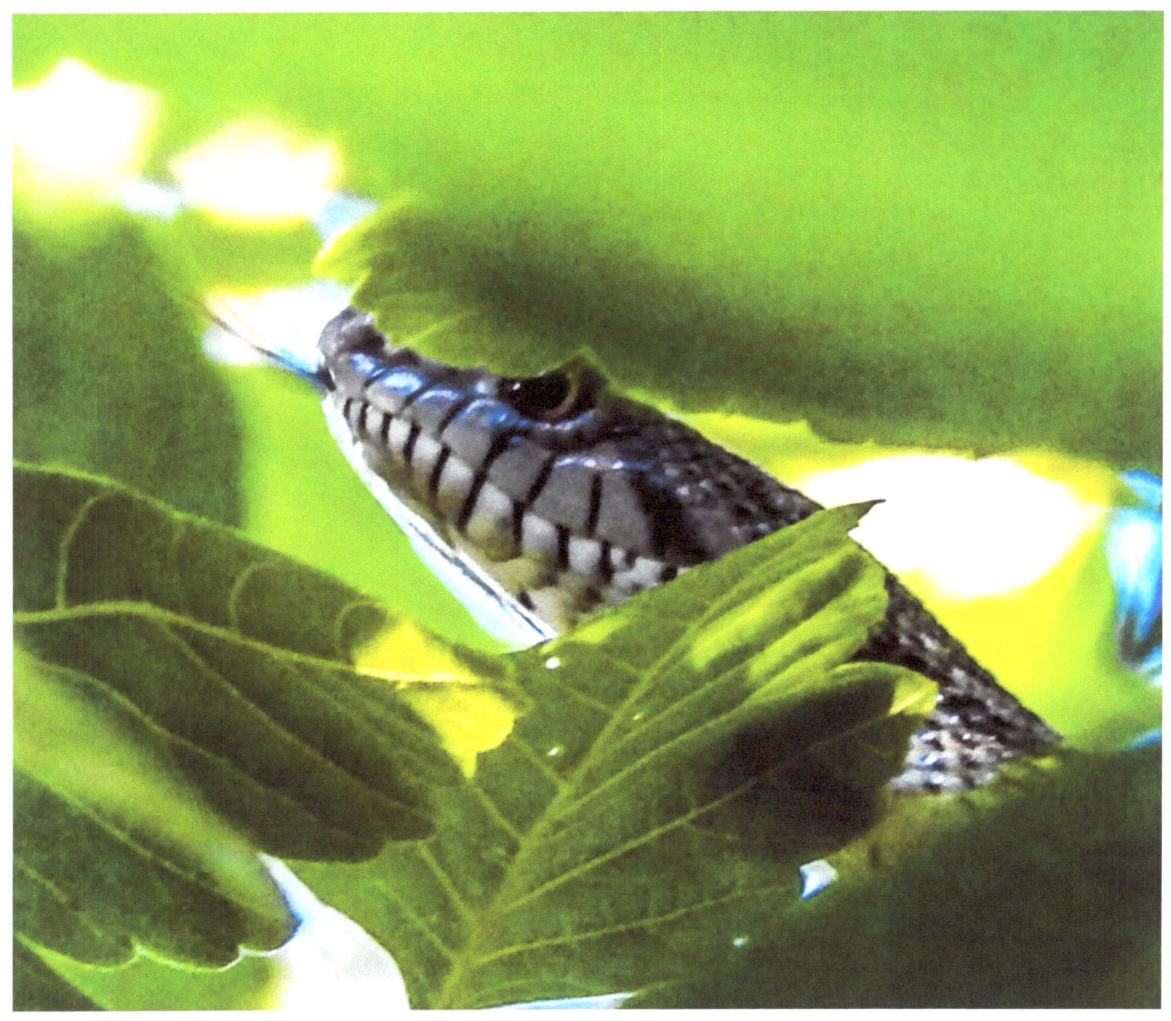

Notice the action of the forked tongue. It gathers molecules in the saliva and tastes the air in much the same way that humans sniff the air.

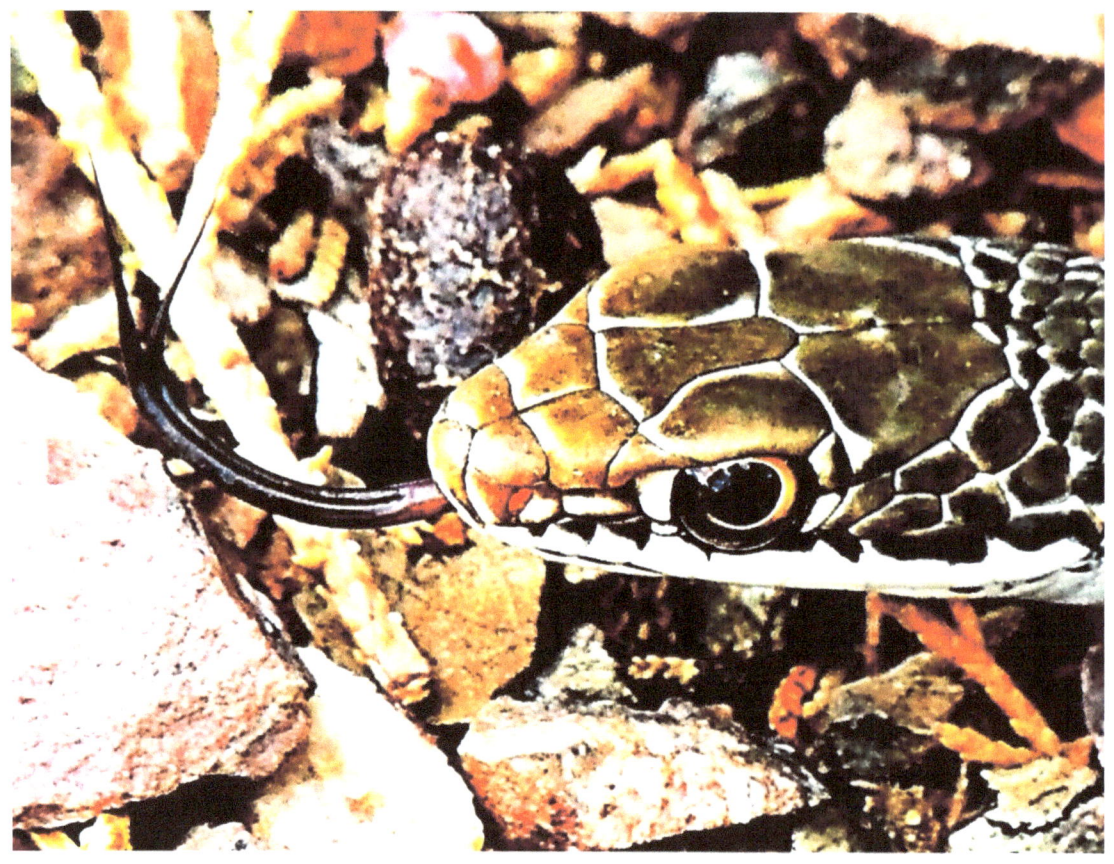

Note the groove in the tongue. This is evidently to channel the saliva back to the Jacobson's Organ that detects the molecules collected by the tongue.

MOUNTAIN (HERNANDEZ'S) SHORT-HORNED LIZARD

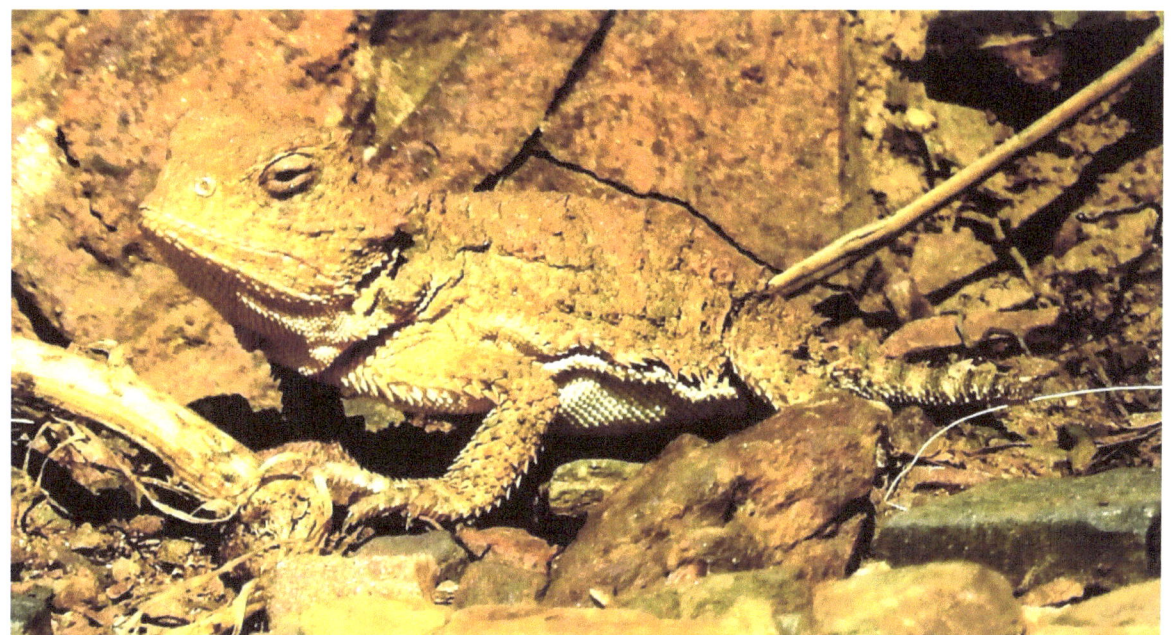

If there is anything that is perfectly camouflaged, this is it. Commonly, but incorrectly, called a horned or horny toad, this is indeed a lizard.

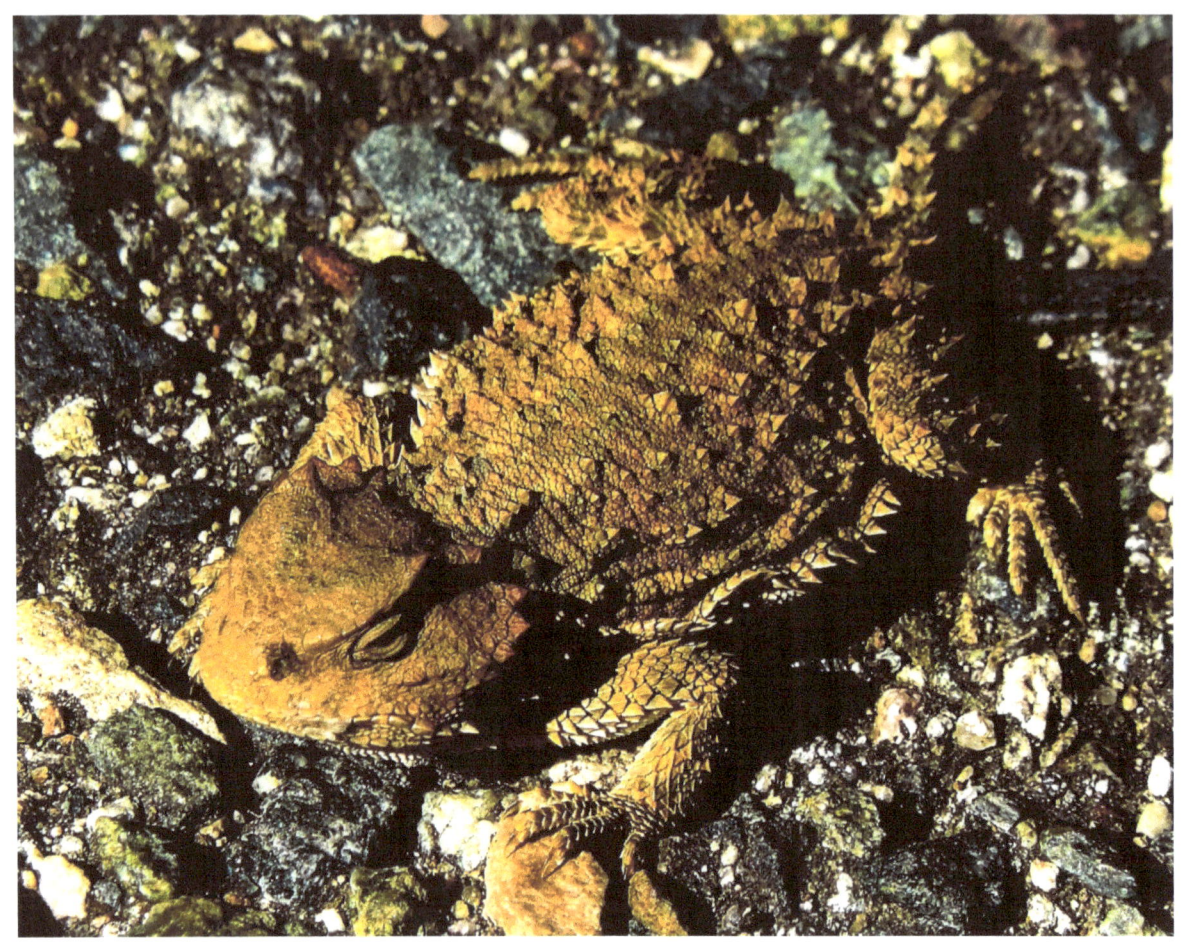

Note how all of the scales have their point toward the back. This makes it harder for a predator to swallow it tail-first. They do not move very fast so they depend on defensive mechanisms.

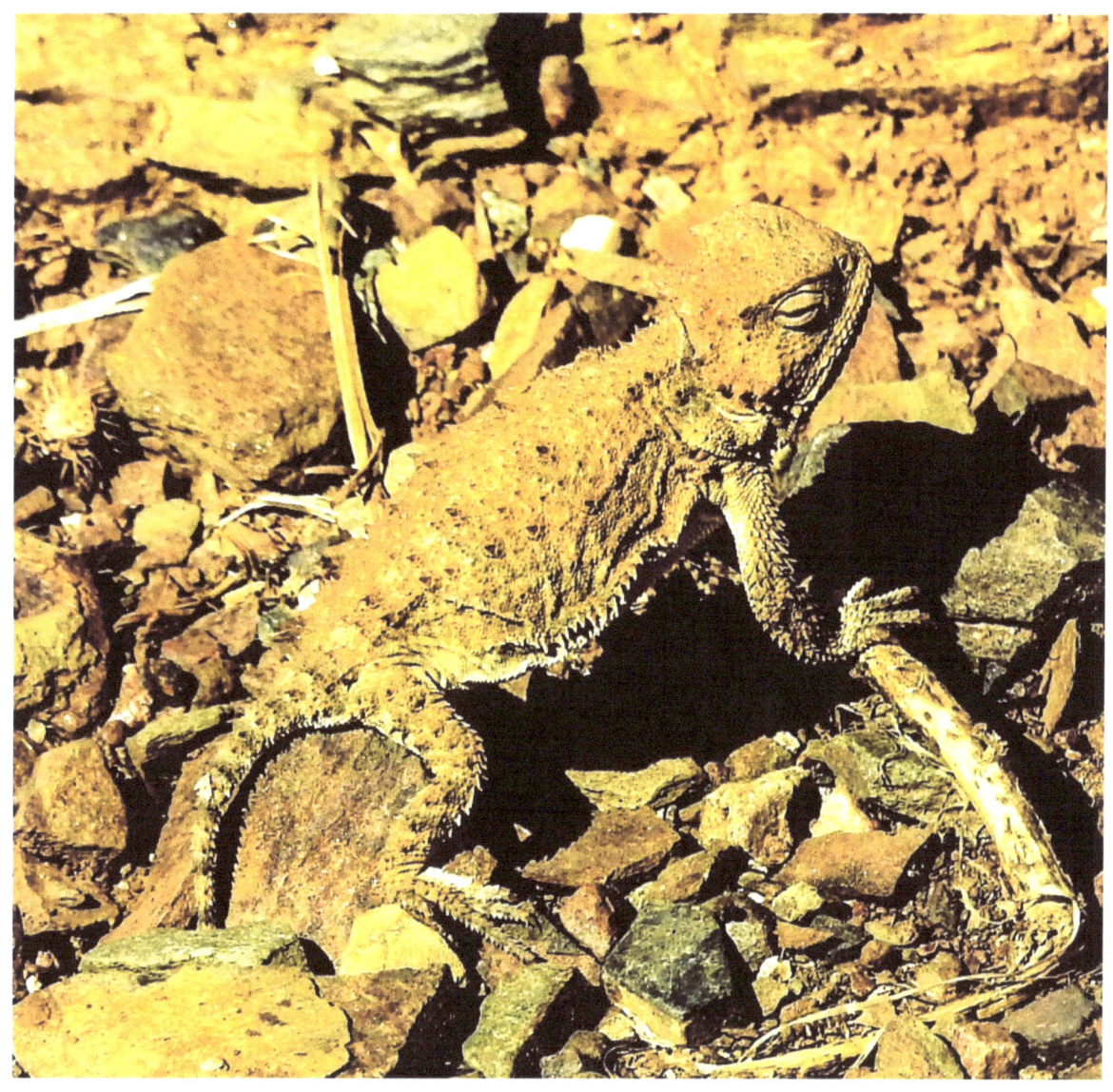

Note the relatively short tail for a lizard. They do not require a longer tail because they are not fast moving. They prefer to sit-and-wait for their prey to come to them catching it with a flick of the tongue.

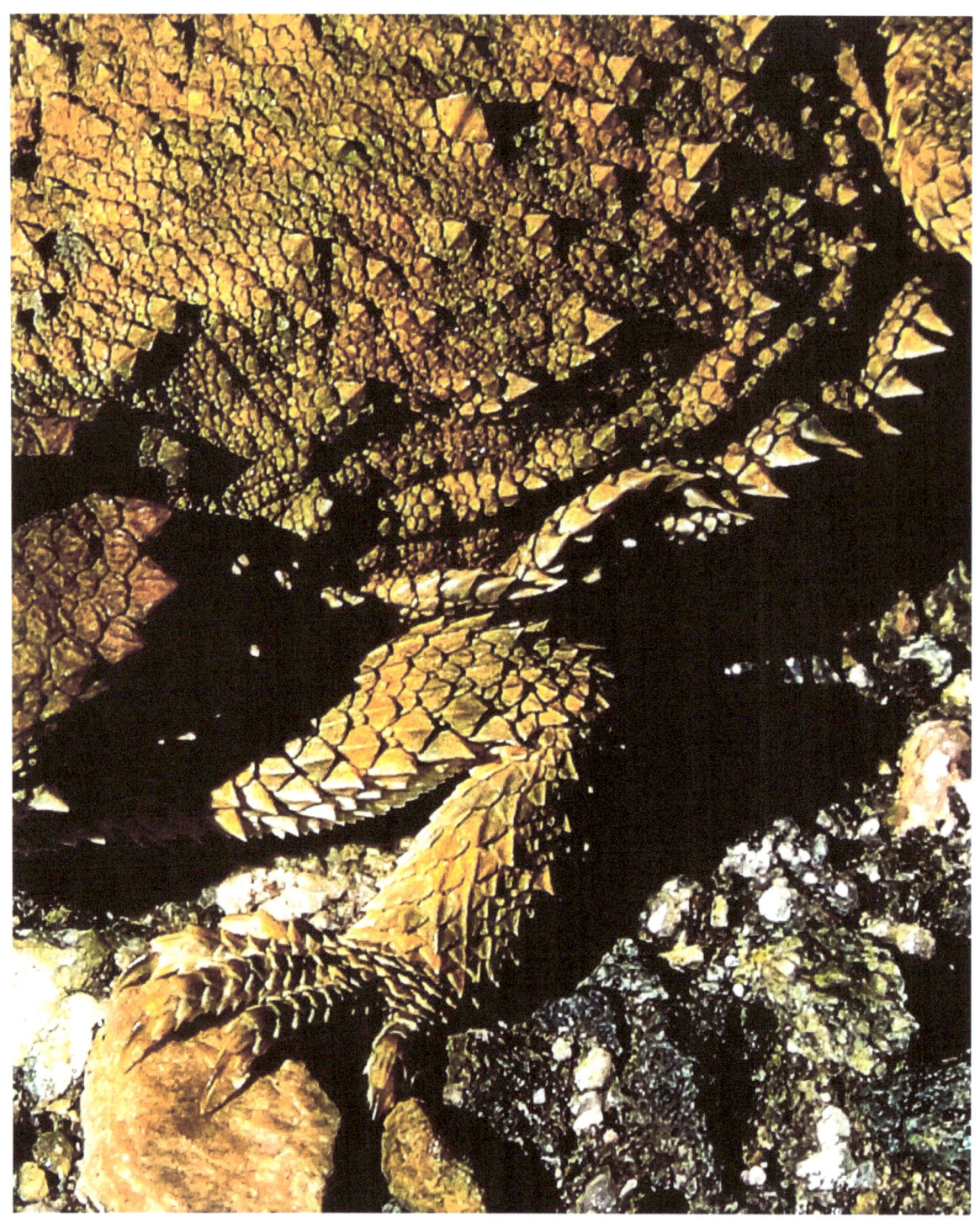

This close-up shows the detail of the left front foot and side. The pattern of the scales is also thought to provide an irregular shadow to add to the camouflage.

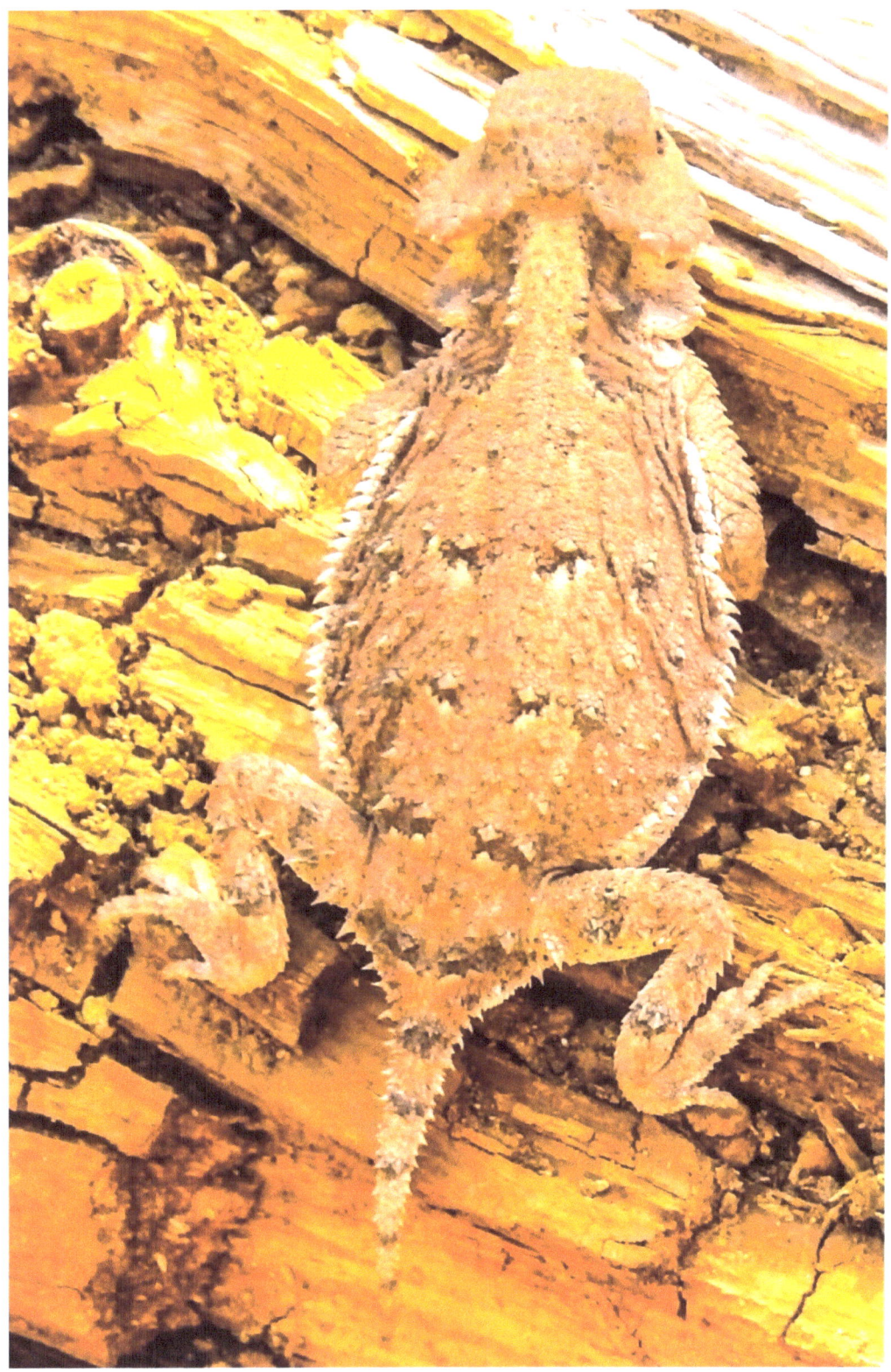

This shows the posture of the horned lizard while waiting for an ant to come along. They feed mostly on ants and mainly during daylight. They are one of the first lizards to come out in the morning.

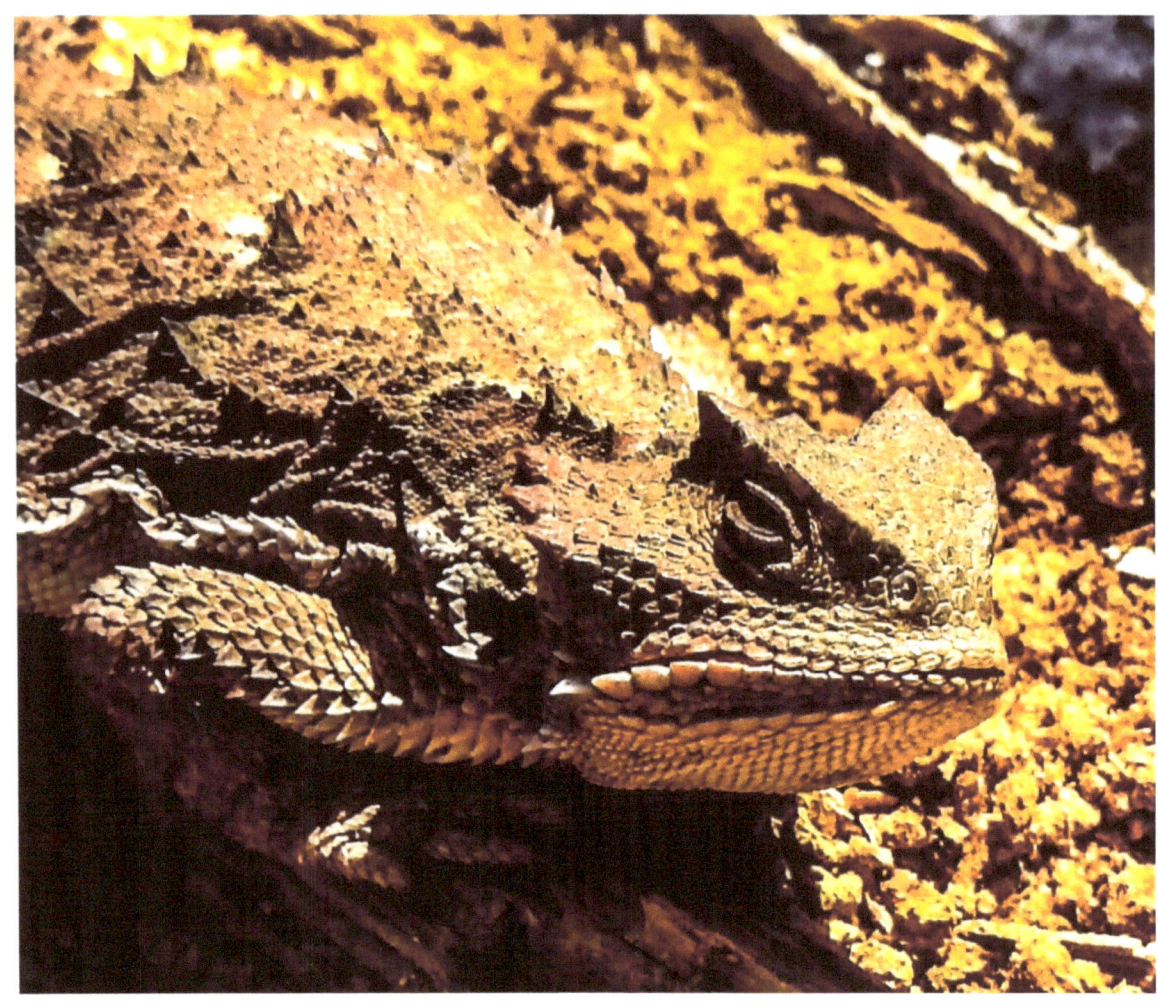

Here you see the detail of the head and back. This species has the ability to squirt blood from an organ behind its eye. It usually reserves this for coyotes and dogs that venture too closely.

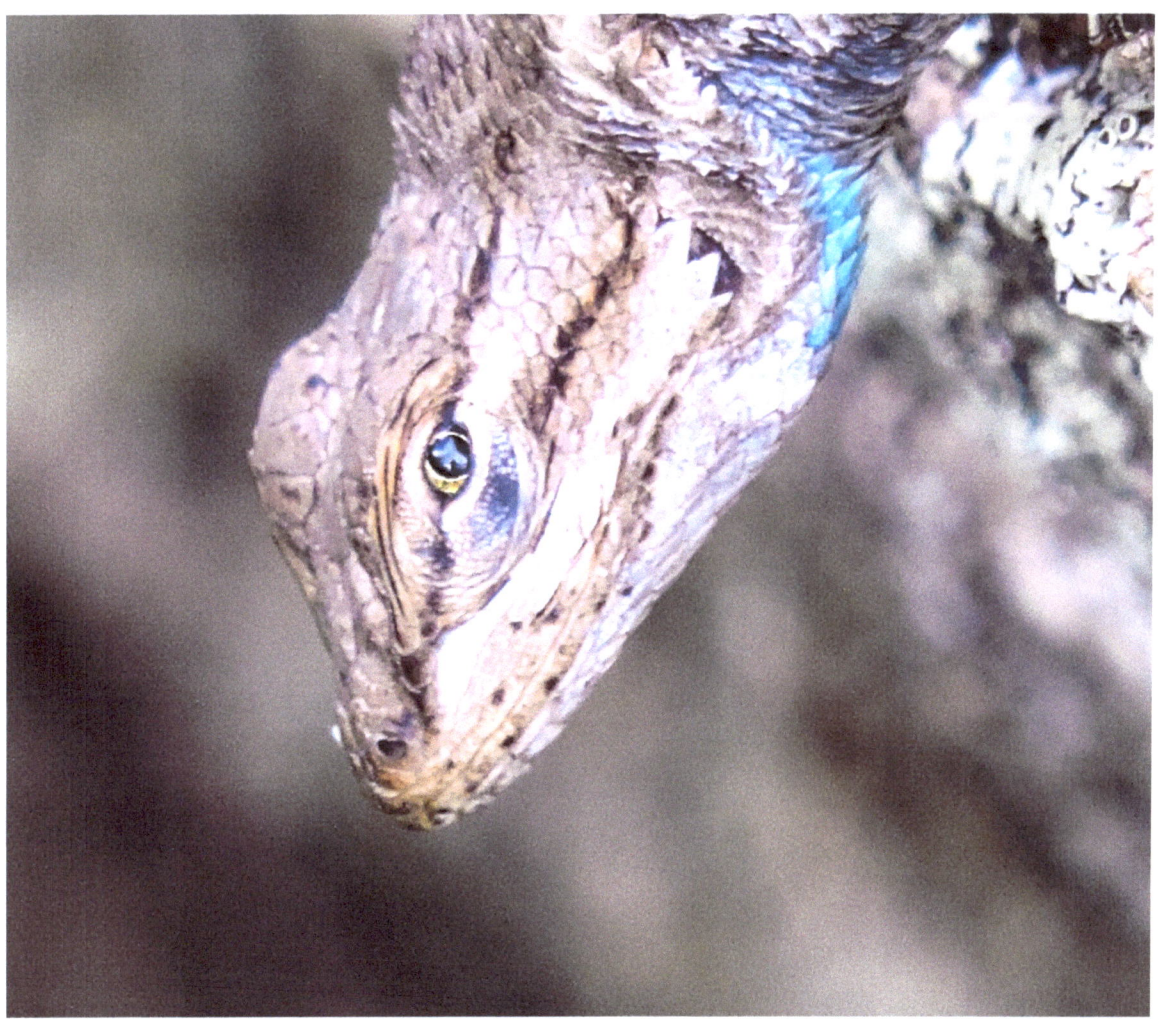

Only the adult males exhibit the blue throat and belly. They need to be camouflaged against flying predators so they are not brightly colored on the back. For dominance displays they do push-ups.

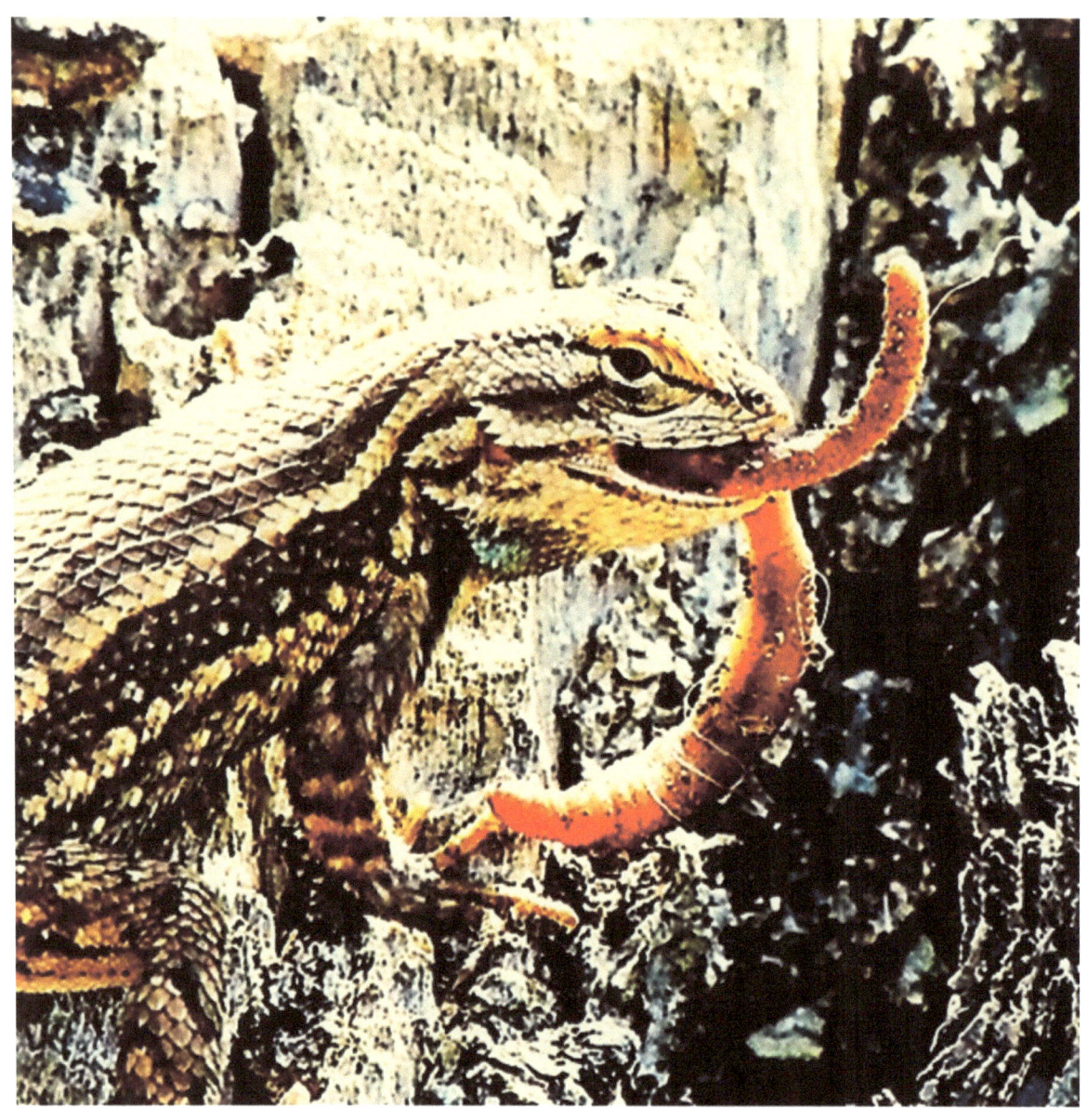

They will eat almost anything that they can catch. However, this male took one chomp on the grub and spit it out. The grub rolled one way and the lizard went the other.

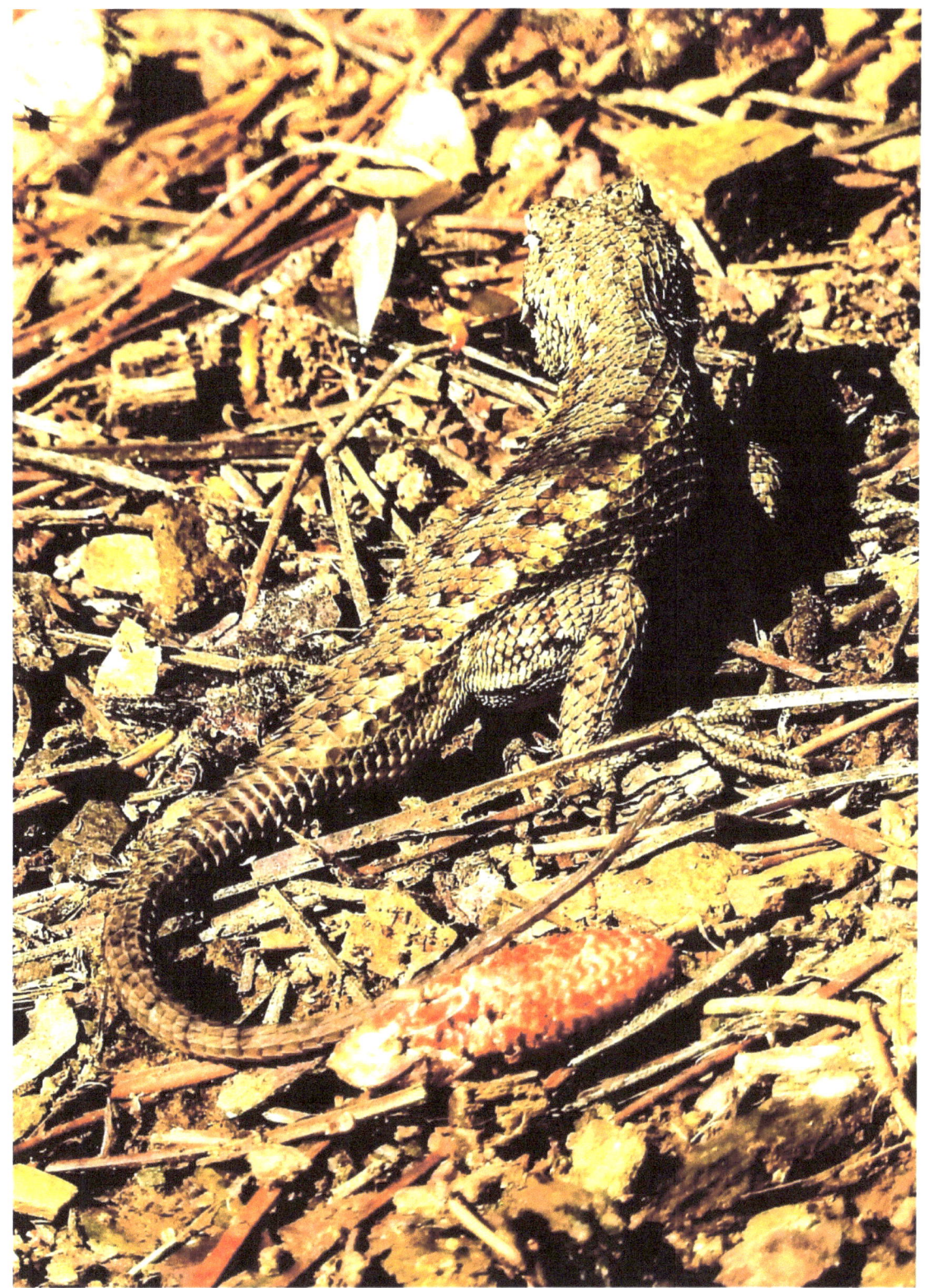

Since these are fast moving lizards they need long tails for counterbalance. If a predator grabs the tail, it will break off and flop around giving the lizard a chance to escape.

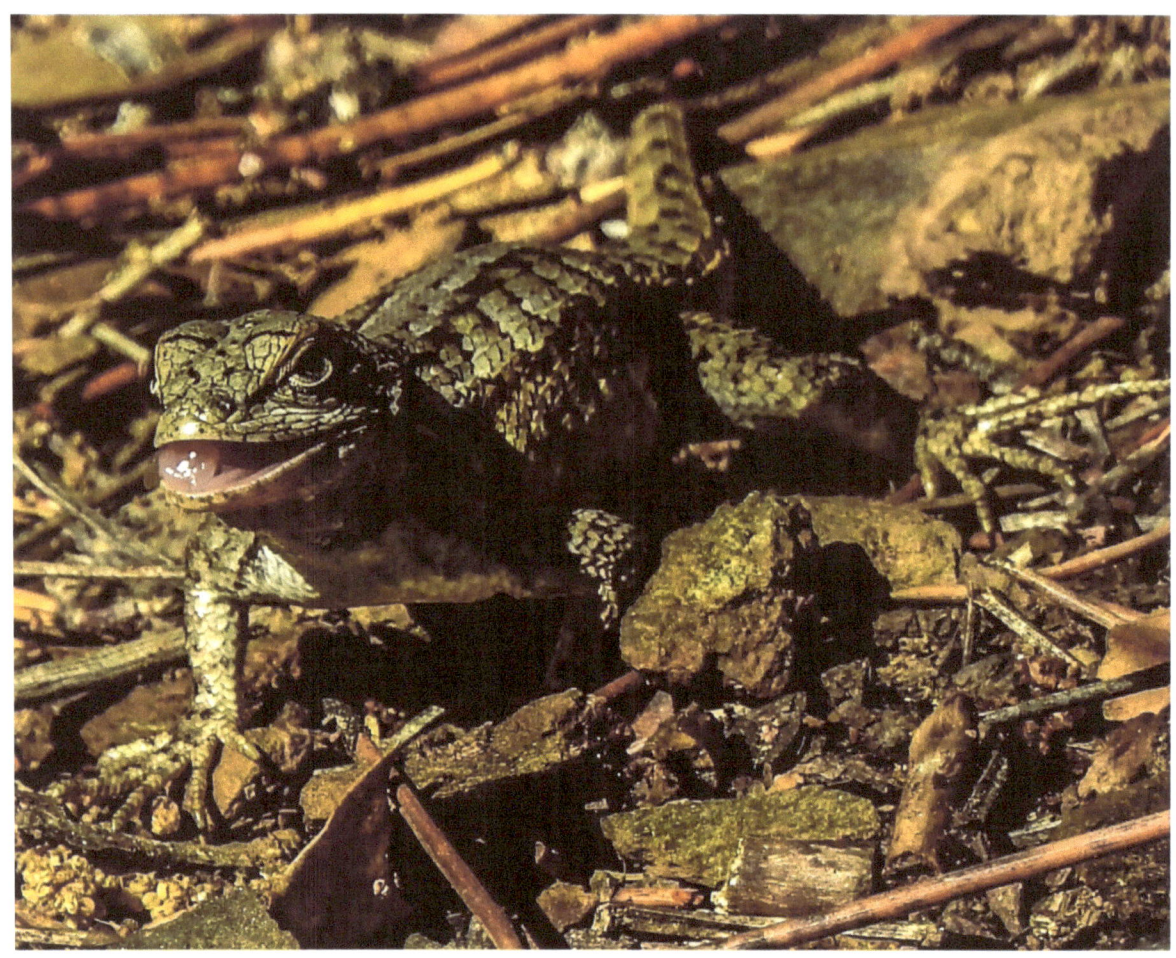

This is a female or juvenile because it does not have the blue belly. It has a termite wing in its mouth. As the termites were emerging from the ground in the spring the lizards were having a feast.

DESERT STRIPED WHIPTAIL

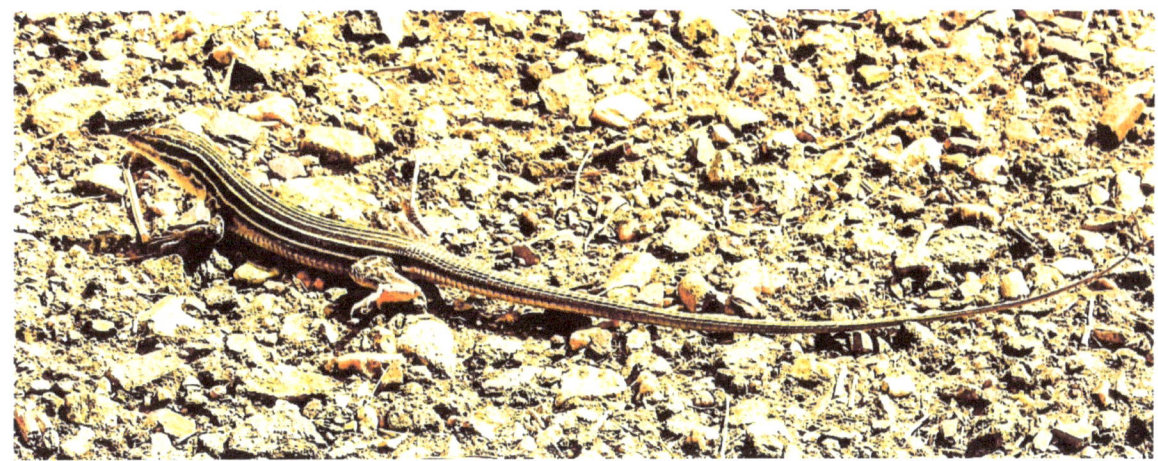

This is an interesting lizard because its tail is about the same length as the rest of its body. It moves very fast so it requires a great amount of counterbalance.

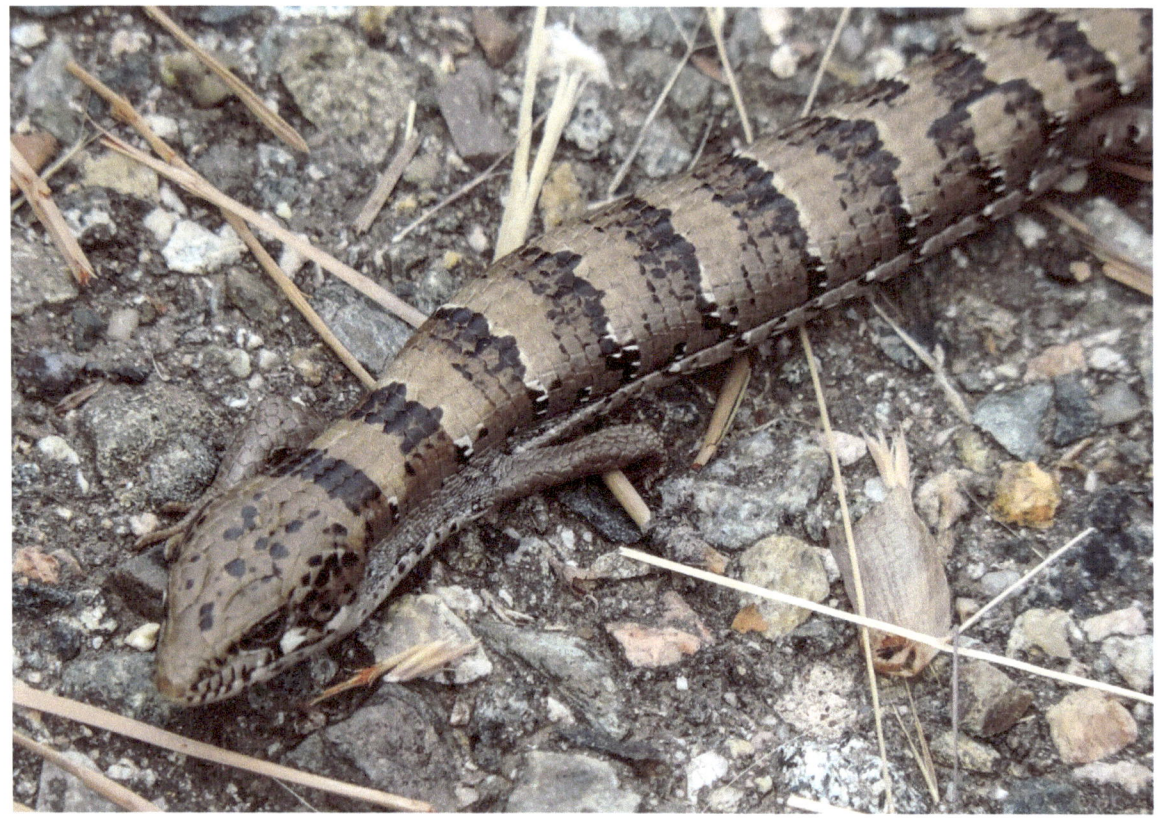

These lizards strongly resemble snakes because their short legs are set well back on their body and as you can see in this picture they can be inconspicuous.

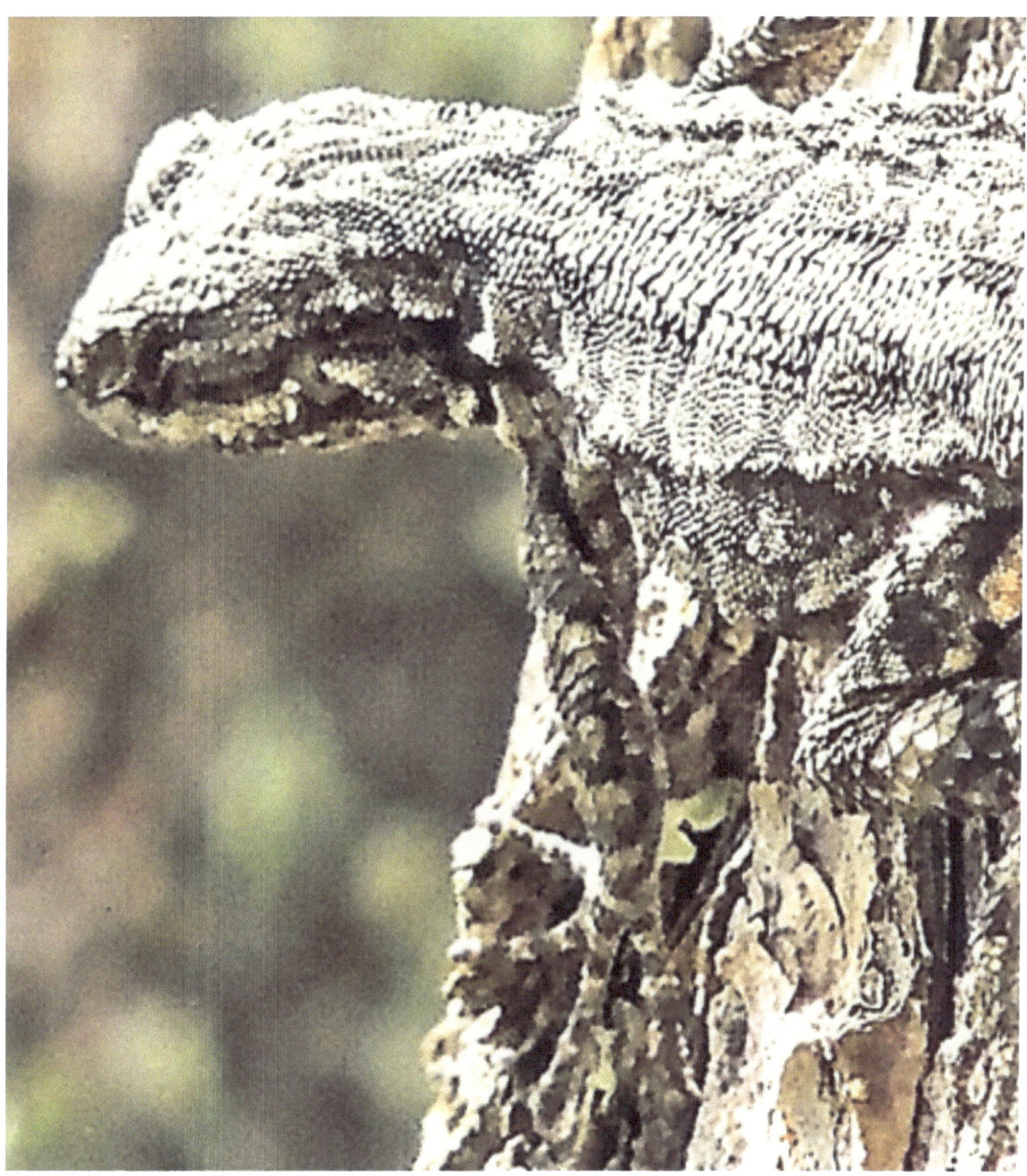

As the name implies, you are more likely to find this lizard on the trunk of a tree than on the ground. The broken pattern of the scales makes excellent camouflage when on a Pinyon Pine tree.

COLLARED LIZARD

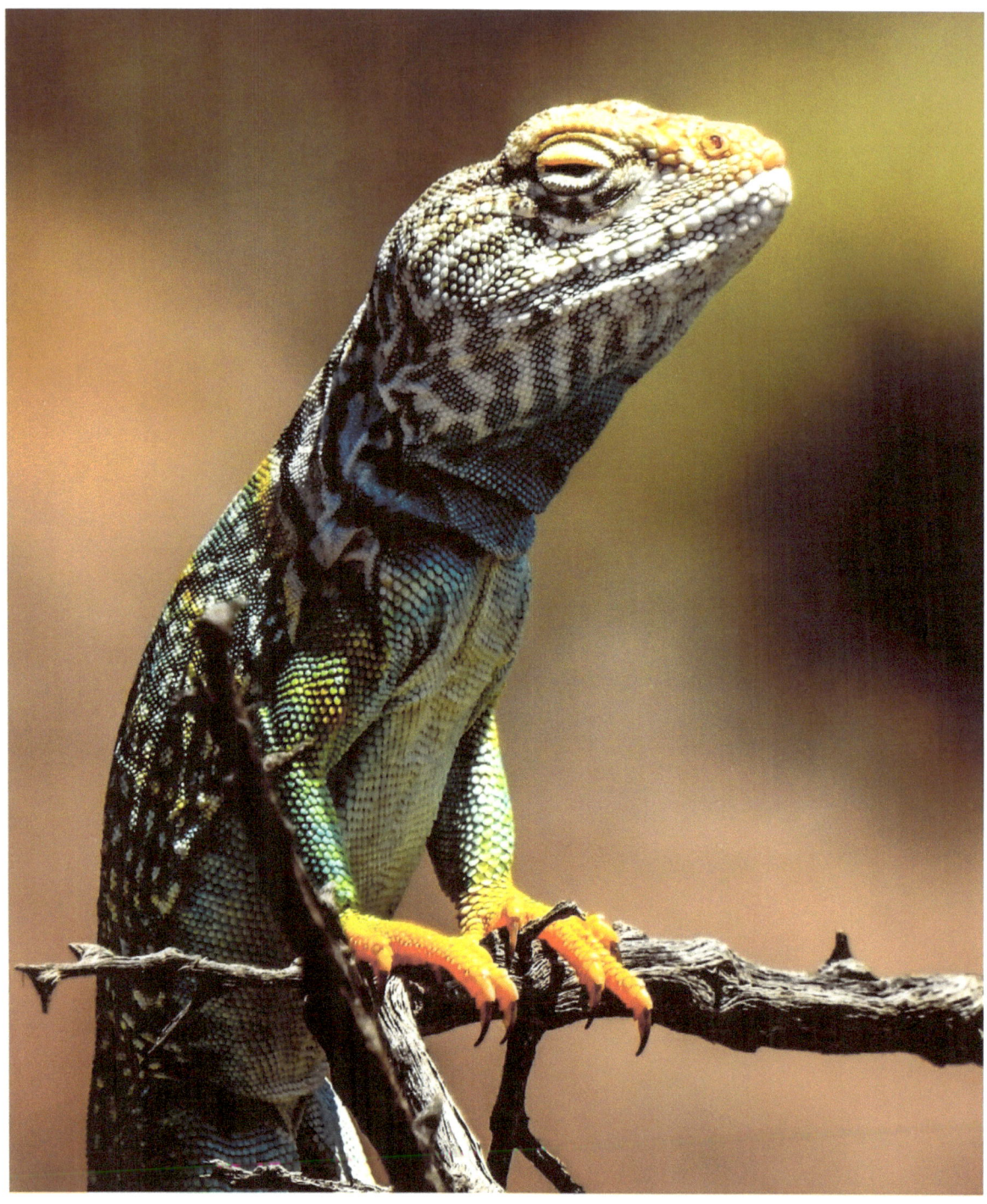

The coloration on this lizard identifies it as a male. Females are a much more drab brown. They prefer hot places – at least 80° and up to 110° F. They eat mainly insects.

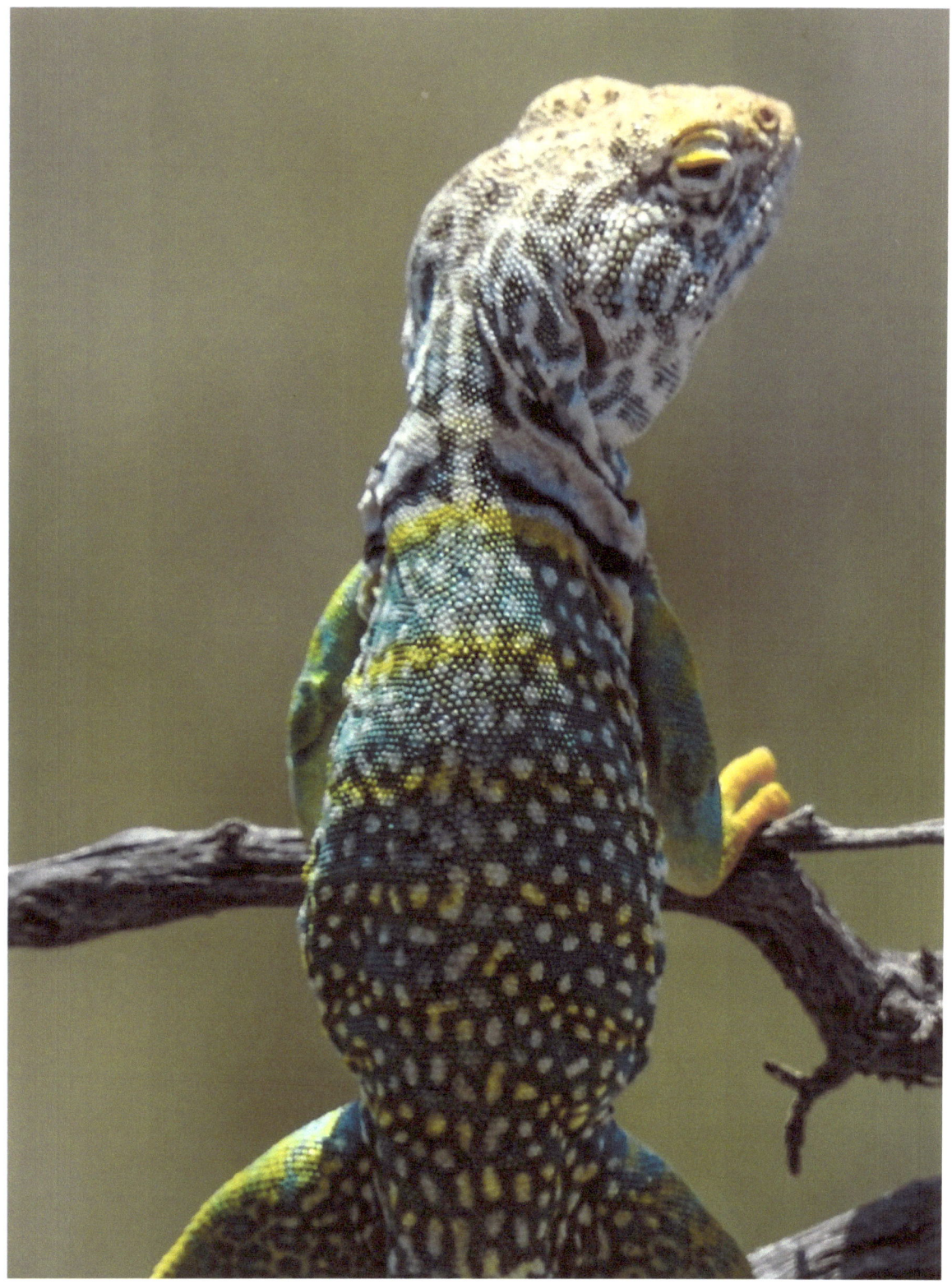

Collared Lizards can run on their hind legs but I have never seen one do so. You could make a dramatic presentation if you depicted one doing this.

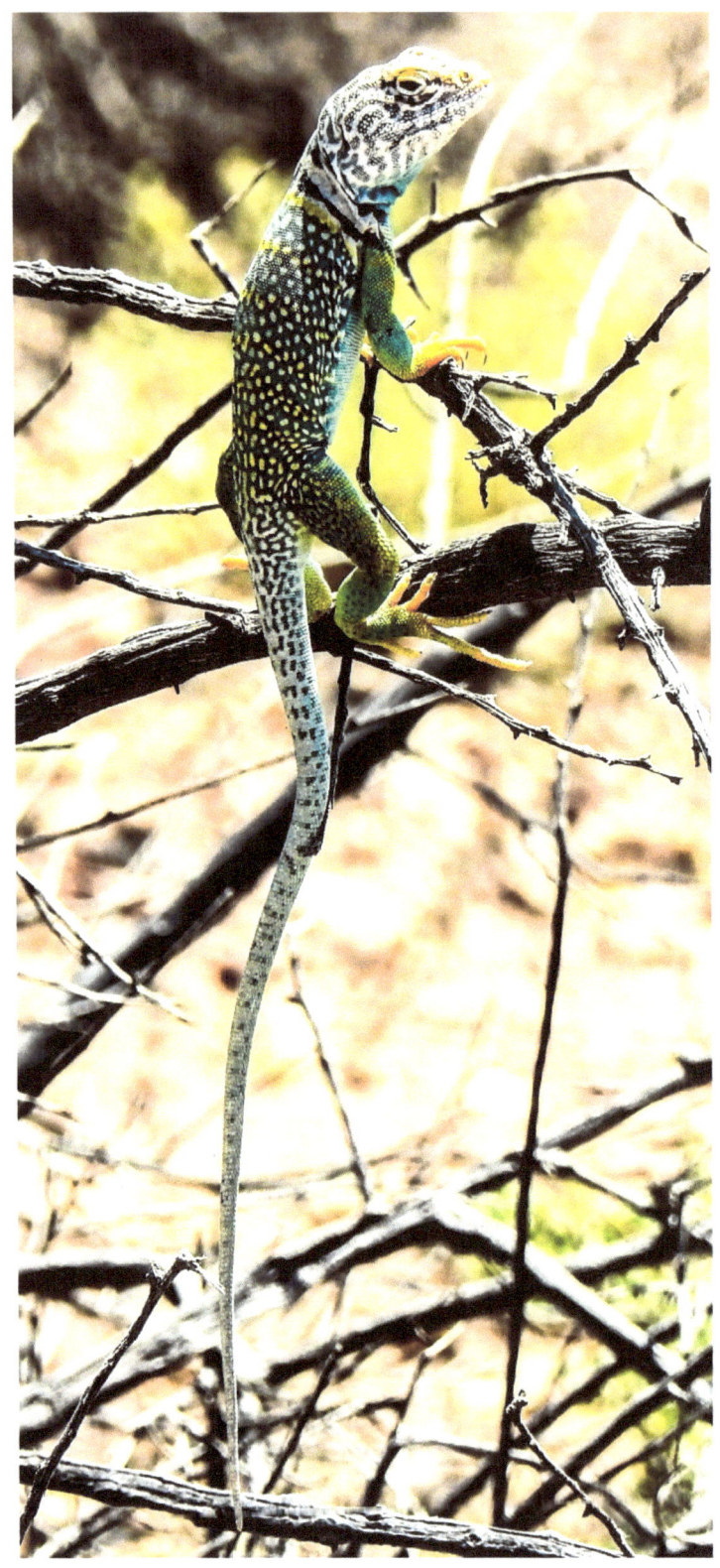

Collard Lizards can grow up to 14' long. Some have been kept as pets but they need heat, a lot of room to run, calcium supplementation and a source of UVB light.

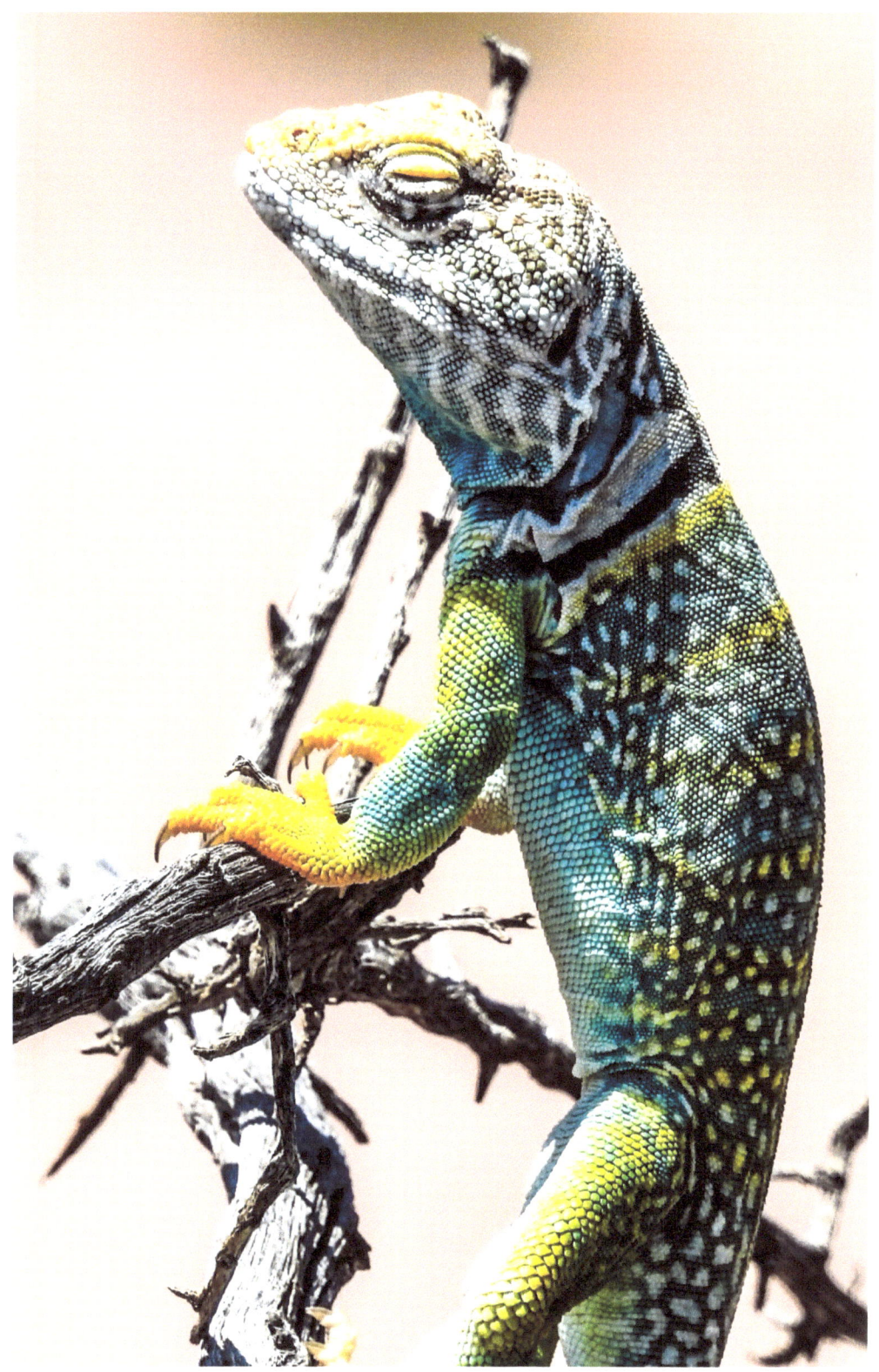

In some areas they are called "mountain boomers" but it is unclear why. They are not known to make any sounds.

www.ingramcontent.com/pod-product-compliance
Lightning Source LLC
Chambersburg PA
CBHW050422180526
45159CB00005B/2372